How Artists See

THE ELEMENTS

Earth Air Fire Water

Colleen Carroll

ABBEVILLE KIDS

A DIVISION OF ABBEVILLE PUBLISHING GROUP

New York London

"Painters understand nature and love her and teach us to see her."

—VINCENT VAN GOGH

This book is dedicated to my brother and sister, Michael and Mary Ann.

I'd like to thank the many people who helped make this book happen, especially Jackie Decter, Ed Decter, Colleen Mohyde, and as always, my husband, Mitch Semel.

—COLLEEN CARROLL

JACKET AND COVER FRONT: N.C. Wyeth, *The Giant,* 1923 (see also pages 12–13).
JACKET AND COVER BACK, LEFT: Red Grooms, *Ploughed Earth* (detail), 1977 (see also pages 6–7); RIGHT: Arthur Dove, *Fire in a Sauerkraut Factory* (detail), 1941, (see also pages 20–21).
JACKET BACK, BOTTOM: Katsushika Hokusai, *In the Well of the Great Wave off Kanagawa* (detail), 1823–29 (see also pages 28–29).

EDITOR: Jacqueline Decter
DESIGNER: Patricia Fabricant
PRODUCTION EDITOR: Abigail Asher
PRODUCTION MANAGER: Lou Bilka

First library edition
10 9 8 7 6 5

Library of Congress Cataloging-in-Publication Data
Carroll, Colleen.
The elements : earth, air, fire, water / Colleen Carroll.
p. cm. — (How artists see, ISSN 1083-821X)
Includes bibliographical references.
Summary: Examines how the four elements have been depicted in works of art from different time periods and places.
ISBN 978-0-7892-0476-9;
1. Four elements (Philosophy) in art—Juvenile literature. [1. Four elements (Philosophy) in art. 2. Art appreciation.]
I. Title. II. Series: Carroll, Colleen. How artists see.
N8217.F68C37 1996
760'.01—dc20 95-43525

For bulk and premium sales and for text adoption procedures, write to Customer Service Manager, Abbeville Press, 137 Varick Street, New York, NY 10013, or call 1-800-ARTBOOK.
Visit Abbeville Press online at www.abbeville.com.

CONTENTS

EARTH

PLOUGHING IN THE NIVERNAIS REGION

by Rosa Bonheur

A long time ago people thought the world was made up of four things: earth, air, fire, and water. They called these things the elements. Ever since then, artists have tried to capture their power and beauty. As you turn the pages of this book you will see some of the many different ways that artists see the elements.

This realistic picture shows farmers and pairs of oxen plowing a field in France on a bright, sunny day. It's so lifelike that you can almost smell the fresh clumps of soil that have just been turned and feel their weight in your hand. If you look closely at the newly plowed earth, you can see dark patches in between the small mounds of soil. What do you think these dark patches are?

The oxen march in a diagonal line across the field. Trace your finger along the line of oxen from the smallest one to the biggest. How quickly do you think they move? Can you find any other straight lines in the picture?

PLOUGHED EARTH

by Red Grooms

Here's a more playful version of the same subject. In this picture, a farmer takes a break after plowing the field with a tractor. The artist uses dabs and lines of paint to show the turned rows of earth. Trace your finger over the clumps of soil to get a sense of how the artist applied the paint. Now look back at the brown earth in *Ploughing in the Nivernais Region.* How have the artists painted the two fields differently?

These lucky horses aren't working but lazily grazing on left-over bits of hay. If you look carefully, you'll see that the biggest horse seems to stick out from the flat surface of the picture. To create this three-dimensional effect, the artist made the horse and other objects in the picture from separate pieces of wood, and then attached them to the painted field. Can you find other parts of the picture that are made this way?

EARTH

SPRING TURNING

by Grant Wood

Have you ever seen the earth from an airplane or the top of a very tall building? What did it look like? In this view of the earth, a series of gently rolling hills reaches far into the distance, and objects appear smaller than they actually are. Point to the tiny farmer tilling the soil. What other things can you find tucked into the landscape?

The artist has shown the earth as a patchwork quilt of bright greens and deep browns to celebrate the arrival of spring. Move your finger around the brown rectangles of plowed earth.

If you were standing on the ground, this rectangular pattern would look quite different. How do you think it would change?

LANDSCAPE NO. 3

by Marsden Hartley

Here's another painting that shows the earth from a distance, only this time the view is of great, bumpy mountains instead of softly rounded hills. What other things in the picture have similar curving shapes? The mountains are so big that they dwarf the adobe brick houses in the valley. These houses are the only things in the picture made out of straight lines. Can you find them?

The artist created this rugged landscape out of many patches of paint. What colors can you find? Which ones most resemble the color of the earth? The artist chose these colors to help you feel what it's like to be in this particular place. If you could jump inside this painting, what do you think the weather would be like?

THE GIANT

by N. C. Wyeth

Air may be the hardest of all the elements for artists to capture because, as you know, air is invisible. So artists sometimes show the effect air has on things that you *can* see. To show the air in this painting of a breezy day at the beach, the artist includes sea gulls with flapping wings, the spray of the surf, and children with windswept hair. What else do you see in the sky?

Cloudy days are the perfect time to "see" air, because it's air that makes clouds move across the sky. Trace your finger around the purple cloud giant. How quickly do you think he's moving? Where might he be going? The next time you are cloud watching, maybe you, too, will see a giant or some other amazing creature.

ONCOMING SPRING

by Charles Burchfield

This artist liked to show the power of the weather. Here, the last cold winds of winter whip through the trees with such force that they bend the trunks and shake the branches. With your finger, trace the yellow shapes that show the force of the air rushing through the woods. If you were in this forest, what sounds

might you hear? Use your voice to make the sound of this wintry wind.

The artist used watercolor paints to capture the slushy wetness of melting snow and the overcast skies of the changing season. Move your finger along the snow bank at the bottom of the picture to see how the artist blended the colors. How much longer do you think it will be before spring comes to these woods?

STUDY OF CLOUDS

by John Constable

To show the invisible element in action, this artist made many sketches and paintings of clouds that seem to shift and glide across the sky on the changing air currents. Look at the patch of dark clouds at the bottom of the picture. What do you think will happen if these ominous clouds settle over the countryside?

In this picture the artist painted the clouds in a free, loose way, as if he was working quickly to capture them before they had a chance to float away. Look back at *The Giant.* How have these two artists shown the sky differently? Which clouds seem to be moving faster?

SKY ABOVE CLOUDS, IV

by Georgia O'Keeffe

Birds see something like this view of the sky all the time, and people see it from airplanes and even from space ships. As a matter of fact, the artist made this painting after taking a ride in an airplane. The white clouds seem to float on the air like lily pads on a still, blue pond. What else do these clouds remind you of?

You may have noticed that the clouds get smaller and the colors get lighter as your eye meets the pink horizon line. The artist did this to show space and distance. You've probably seen these pale colors in the sky before. What time of day do you think the artist is trying to show? If you were in an airplane flying over this neat pattern of clouds, how many miles do you think it would be from the biggest clouds to the very smallest ones?

FIRE IN A SAUERKRAUT FACTORY

by Arthur Dove

Fire is an element that's mysterious, beautiful, and scary all at the same time. And because fire doesn't have an exact shape, it can be a very difficult thing for an artist to capture. In this painting the flames are thick bands of intense color that reach toward the sky and fill up the whole canvas. Vibrant flames of red, orange, pink, and yellow burst from the white heat of the fire's core. Which color looks the hottest to you?

This raging fire burns with violent energy. The artist applied the paint in curving lines to show how the flames writhe and leap out of control. Trace your finger over all the lines to experience the fire's furious movement. With your body, show the dancing motion of twisting flames.

BURNING OF THE HOUSES OF PARLIAMENT

by Joseph Mallord William Turner

A burning building is truly an awesome, terrifying sight to behold, as you see in this picture of a historical event. Point to the burning building. The orange, yellow, and red flames light up the sky and cast reflections on the water. How does the fire look different from its reflection? A crowd of people stand in the shadows on the opposite riverbank and watch the blaze from a safe distance. Do you think they can feel the heat of this great fire?

Look back at *Fire in a Sauerkraut Factory.* Both of these pictures show buildings consumed by fire, yet they are very different. Which painting seems more realistic to you? Which fire do you think is more powerful and frightening?

APACHE MEDICINE SONG

by Frederic Remington

People have been gathering around campfires to talk, tell stories, sing, and warm themselves for thousands of years. Here, the artist doesn't show the flames of the fire, just a wisp of smoke and an orange light that gives the scene a warm glow. Point to the places where you see the firelight.

Outside of the circle of light, night has fallen on the campsite. The dark shadows surrounding the bright fire give the picture a mysterious mood as the men sing their song. What do you think their music sounds like?

FALLING ROCKET

by James Abbott McNeill Whistler

This festive painting shows the moment after fireworks have exploded, leaving only the falling sparks. The artist used dabs of bright paint to capture the sparkling bits of light as they drift toward the ground. Starting at the top of the picture, run your finger along the trail of sparks. How quickly do you think they fall?

Even though it's night-time, the light created by the fireworks is bright enough to cast a faint glow on the scene and illuminate the shadowy forms of the people watching from across the river. As soon as the sparks disappear, the areas of gray paint that seem to hang in the sky will be all that remains. What do you think they are?

WATER

IN THE WELL OF THE GREAT WAVE OFF KANAGAWA

by Katsushika Hokusai

Did you know that three-quarters of the earth is covered by water? You'll find water in rivers, lakes, streams, and ponds, but most of the earth's water lies in the great oceans. This picture shows huge ocean waves off the coast of Japan. Point to the narrow boats tucked in between the waves. Why do you think the artist made the boats and people so small and the waves so big?

The water seems to be alive with its foamy claws and wide, hungry mouth, and the people have to row furiously to keep from being swallowed up. The artist used strong, curving lines to capture the power and energy of the waves. Would you want to be on a boat in these rough waters?

THE STEERSMAN

by Théo van Rysselberghe

Here's another picture of a sailor on a choppy sea. Look closely, and you will see that the artist applied the paint in small dots. The blue, green, and white dots of the water look like the misty spray of the ocean.

Use your finger to trace the movement of the waves as they swell and break.

The sailor looks calm and confident as he steers his craft through the rough water.

Now look back at *In the Well of the Great Wave Off Kanagawa.* Both pictures show people navigating their vessels over perilous waters. Which of the boats would you rather be on?

A BIGGER SPLASH

by David Hockney

Have you ever jumped into a refreshing pool of water on a hot summer day? If you have, you'll be able to tell what has just happened in this picture. Trace your finger over the water that splashes above the surface. What colors did the artist use to create the splash? How does it look different from the still water?

You might have to put on your sunglasses to look at the vivid shades of pink, yellow, and blue that the artist has chosen. Sometimes artists use color to create certain feelings or to set a mood. Which colors feel hot? Which ones feel cool? Do the colors in this picture make you want to take a dip?

WATER

LES NYMPHÉAS BLANCS (THE WHITE WATERLILIES)

by Claude Monet

The pond in this picture of a lush garden is a quiet home to many types of living things, including the waterliles that float in clusters on its surface. So many plants fill the pond that the dark water is almost completely covered. In between the flowers, there are brush strokes of green, white, and yellow paint. What do you think they represent? If you were looking into the water, what would you see?

Now that you've discovered how some artists see the elements, use your own special way of seeing to make a picture of earth, air, fire, or water.

NOTE TO PARENTS AND TEACHERS

As an elementary school teacher I had the opportunity to show my students many examples of great art. I was always amazed by their enthusiastic responses to the colors, shapes, subjects, and fascinating stories of the artists' lives. It wasn't uncommon for us to spend twenty minutes looking at and talking about just one work of art. By asking challenging questions, I prompted the children to examine and think very carefully about the art, and then quite naturally they would begin to ask all sorts of interesting questions of their own. These experiences inspired me to write this book and the other volumes in the *How Artists See* series.

How Artists See is designed to teach children about the world by looking at art, and about art by looking at the world through the eyes of great artists. The books encourage children to look critically, answer—and ask—thought-provoking questions, and form an appreciation and understanding of an artist's vision. Each book is devoted to a single subject, so that children can see how different artists have approached and treated the same theme, and begin to understand the importance of individual style.

Because I believe that children learn most successfully in an atmosphere of exploration and discovery, I've included questions that encourage them to formulate ideas and responses for themselves.

And because people's reactions to art are based on their own personal aesthetic, most of the questions are open-ended and have more than one answer. If you're reading aloud to your children or students, give them ample time to look at each work and form their own opinions; it certainly is not necessary to read the whole book in one sitting. Like a good book or movie, art can be enjoyed over and over again, each time with the possibility of revealing something that wasn't seen before.

You may notice that dates and other historical information are not included in the main text. I purposely omitted this information in order to focus on the art and those aspects of the world it illustrates. For children who want to learn more about the artists whose works appear in the book, short biographies are provided at the end, along with suggestions for further reading and a list of museums where you can see additional works by each artist.

After reading *How Artists See the Elements,* children can do a wide variety of related activities to extend and reinforce all that they've learned. In addition to the simple activities I've suggested throughout the main text, they can make a basic kite and test its aerodynamics on a windy day, write a poem about their favorite element, or explore the plant and animal life of a local marsh, pond, or stream. Since the examples shown here are just a tiny fraction of the great works of art that feature the four elements, children can go on a scavenger hunt through museums and the many wonderful art books in your local library to find other images of earth, air, fire, and water.

I hope that you and your children or students will enjoy reading and rereading this book and, by looking at many styles of art, discover how artists share with us their unique ways of seeing and depicting our world.

ARTISTS' BIOGRAPHIES

(in order of appearance)

If you'd like to know more about the artists in this book, here's some information to get you started:

ROSA BONHEUR (1822–1899), *pp. 4–5*

This French painter and sculptor worked as an artist at a time in history when women weren't encouraged to work outside the home. The daughter of a painter, Rosa Bonheur (pronounced *bone-ER*) was taught that art and artists are an important part of society, and she took her career as a painter quite seriously. Once, in order to be allowed into a horse fair to observe the animals at close range, she had to dress as a man! Rosa Bonheur is known for her large paintings of animals at work and play, and for her landscapes of the French countryside.

RED GROOMS (BORN 1937), *pp. 6–7*

This American artist began to draw as a young boy, and at age ten his mother enrolled him in art classes at the local museum. In the eighth grade his model of a circus won first prize in a hobby fair, and he had his first art exhibit while he was still in high school. From then on, Red Grooms was in and out of art schools, never finding one that could hold his interest. Instead of finishing art school, he moved to New York City, where he began making all kinds of art, including paintings, sculptures, and his famous "constructions," whole scenes that look like miniature theater sets. Some of his favorite subjects are life in New York City and humorous portraits of family and friends.

GRANT WOOD (1892–1942), *pp. 8–9*

While many American painters were off studying art in Europe in the early twentieth century, Grant Wood was busy painting pictures that captured life in the American countryside. This "American Scene" painter is best known for his pictures of farmers at work, rolling green fields, and portraits of people from the American heartland. His painting called *American Gothic* is one of the most popular and recognizable pictures ever made.

MARSDEN HARTLEY (1877–1943), *pp. 10–11*

Along with Arthur Dove (look back at *Fire in a Sauerkraut Factory*), Georgia O'Keeffe (look back at *Sky Above Clouds, IV*), and others, Marsden Hartley was talented and lucky enough to have his work shown at "291," a New York City art gallery that helped start the careers of many young American modern artists. And, like many young painters in the early part of the twentieth century, Hartley traveled to Europe to learn about new and exciting things that were happening there in art. Using what he had learned, he created his own style; his style changed many times throughout his life. One of his favorite subjects was the rocky landscape of Maine, which he painted over and over again.

NEWELL CONVERS (N. C.) WYETH (1882–1945), *pp. 12–13*

As a boy growing up on a Massachusetts farm, N. C. Wyeth (pronounced *WHY-ith*) liked to draw the nature that he saw all around him. His mother noticed his talent and sent him to art school, even though his father wanted him to be a farmer's apprentice. As a young illustrator, Wyeth traveled to the western United States so he could see the subjects that interested him most: cowboys, animals, and Native Americans. At age twenty-one he sold his first illustration, a picture of a cowboy on a bucking bronco. He went on to illustrate many classic children's stories, including *Treasure Island, Robin Hood, The Last of the Mohicans,* and *The Yearling*. Wyeth was also an easel painter, and toward the end of his life he painted many beautiful still lifes and landscapes of the countryside around his home in Pennsylvania. This great American illustrator was the father of the famous painter Andrew Wyeth.

CHARLES BURCHFIELD (1893–1967), *pp. 14–15*

"There is nothing in nature that will ever fail to interest me." The artist who spoke these words was Charles Burchfield, an American watercolor painter who loved the outdoors and the natural world. Many of his paintings show the sides of nature that most people would rather not have to deal with, such as rain- and snowstorms. To Charles Burchfield, everything that happened in nature was a source of wonder, and he tried to capture this feeling in his paintings. Some of his favorite subjects were changing seasons, starry nights, and landscapes filled with blowing grasses and flowers in bloom.

JOHN CONSTABLE (1776–1837), *pp. 16–17*

This English landscape painter tried to show nature exactly as he saw it. To do this, he first made oil sketches out-of-doors and then went back to his studio to create the final painting. Constable was very interested in sunlight, wind, and air, and many of his paintings have huge skies filled with beautiful white clouds. He was so taken with clouds that he made hundreds of cloud "studies" in order to learn how to paint them perfectly. Many later artists, such as Claude Monet (look back at *Les Nymphéas Blancs*), were inspired by Constable's art as they developed their own style of painting.

GEORGIA O'KEEFFE (1887–1986), *pp. 18–19*

When the American painter Georgia O'Keeffe was twelve years old, she told a friend that she would become an artist. She went to art school and later became a teacher. When she was twenty-five years old, she sent some of her watercolor paintings to her best friend, who showed them to a gallery owner in New York City. The gallery owner was Alfred Stieglitz, a very famous photographer who would later become her husband. Stieglitz was so impressed with O'Keeffe's pictures that he hung them up in his gallery without even asking her permission! That was the start of her long and amazing career as an artist. Her paintings show ordinary things in unusual ways, such as a single flower that fills up the whole canvas, sun-bleached animal skulls, seashells, and desert hillsides.

ARTHUR DOVE (1880–1946), *pp. 20–21*

In 1907 Arthur Dove traveled to Paris, France, to study painting. When he returned to America, he began to show his paintings at the 291 gallery in New York City. This important gallery held exhibits of young American artists who were taking painting in bold, new directions. Arthur Dove made many paintings of nature. He especially liked to paint pictures of the universe. He called his paintings "abstractions" because in them he changed the way things really look. This great artist was one of the pioneers of modern American painting.

JOSEPH MALLORD WILLIAM TURNER (1775–1851), *pp. 22–23*

Swirling snowstorms, burning buildings, misty sunsets, and driving rain are some of the subjects of J. M. W. Turner's paintings. This English landscape artist was fascinated by the powerful forces of nature and tried to capture them in his work. Before Turner, most landscape artists tried to make their pictures look as real as possible. Turner's style is just the opposite.

He applied paint in a loose way that made his pictures look blurry. Many people found this style quite strange at first, but later artists, such as Monet and the other Impressionists, thought it was brilliant. They learned many lessons from Turner that helped them create their own style of painting.

FREDERIC REMINGTON (1861–1909), *pp. 24–25*

After the American Civil War (1861–65) many artists headed west along with thousands of other people who were settling in the new territories. One of these artists was Frederic Remington, an illustrator, painter, and sculptor who was fascinated by life in the wild west. Remington is known for his pictures of cowboys on horseback, Native Americans, and bronze sculptures of bucking broncos. Because his work captures this exciting time in American history, Remington is one of the country's most beloved artists.

JAMES ABBOTT McNEILL WHISTLER (1834–1903), *pp. 26–27*

This American artist lived most of his life in London and Paris, where he worked as a painter and printmaker. Many people disliked Whistler's early paintings because of the loose way he used paint. One art critic even accused him of "flinging a pot of paint" at the canvas. He is best known for his later paintings that use only tones of white, gray, and black, such as the famous portrait of his mother, and for pictures that create moods through light and color.

KATSUSHIKA HOKUSAI (1760–1849), *pp. 28–29*

During Katsushika Hokusai's (pronounced *cat-soo-she-kah hoe-coo-sigh*) lifetime, most Japanese artists came from wealthy families. If people were not born into wealth, they had to show enormous artistic gifts in order to study with the great teachers. Hokusai was just such a person. As a boy he worked in a book shop, and then as a wood engraver's apprentice. He showed such talent that at eighteen he went to study with one of Japan's master artists. He is known for his landscape prints and paintings, especially his many pictures of Japan's Mt. Fuji.

THÉO VAN RYSSELBERGHE (1862–1926), *pp. 30–31*

Théo van Rysselberghe (pronounced *RAY-sell-berg*), a painter and graphic artist from Belgium, studied art as a young man before traveling to

North Africa to paint and draw. After he returned to Europe, he helped form "The Twenty," a group of young artists who wanted to paint in a new, modern way. Later he journeyed to Paris, which at the time was the center of the art world. In Paris he met a man named Georges Seurat, who would change the way he painted pictures. Seurat had developed a new style of painting called Pointillism, which was done by applying paint in small dots of color. The technique so impressed the Belgian that he, too, began painting in this style and asked Seurat to become a member of The Twenty. Because most of Rysselberghe's work is painted this way, today he is known as a follower of Seurat.

DAVID HOCKNEY (BORN 1937), *pp. 32–33*

From his earliest childhood, Hockney loved to draw. In math class, when he was supposed to be doing his lessons, he would draw instead. At age eleven, when this Englishman decided to become an artist, he believed that "anyone was an artist who in his job had to pick up a brush and paint something." At thirteen he sold his first painting, a portrait of his father. After grade school, Hockney went to the Royal College of Art, where he began to form his own personal style. He is known for his paintings of sparkling blue swimming pools, still lifes, and interiors, as well as portraits of friends and collages made from hundreds of photographs. This popular artist lives and works in California, another one of his favorite subjects.

CLAUDE MONET (1840–1926), *pp. 34–35*

After a painting called *Impression: Sunrise* by Claude Monet (pronounced *mo-NAY*) was shown in an art exhibit, he and the other artists in the show became known as Impressionists. This group of French artists made paintings that show how sunlight appears at different times of day, during different seasons of the year, and on many different kinds of objects and surfaces, such as morning light on a river or afternoon light on a stone building. Monet liked to work outdoors, and he painted with small brush strokes of pure color that came right out of the tube. He didn't mix his colors (which was the custom of the day), but let the colors blend together in the viewer's eye. Some of his most famous paintings are of waterlilies, haystacks, and the front of a great cathedral in the French town of Rouen. Monet is known as the founder of Impressionism, the style that began what is now known as modern art.

SUGGESTIONS FOR FURTHER READING

The following children's titles are excellent sources for learning more about the artists presented in this book:

FOR EARLY READERS (AGES 4–7)

Bjork, Christina. *Linnea in Monet's Garden.* New York: R&S Books, 1987.
A little girl named Linnea visits the garden of Claude Monet in the French town of Giverny and learns about his life and art along the way. This title is also available on videotape.

FOR INTERMEDIATE READERS (AGES 8–10)

Mason, Antony. *Monet: An Introduction to the Artist's Life and Work.* Famous Artists series. Hauppauge, N. Y.: Barron's, 1995.
This wonderful reference book provides a wealth of information about the life and work of the French Impressionist painter.

Paint and Painting. Voyages of Discovery series. New York: Scholastic Inc., 1994.
The history and techniques of painting are described in this beautifully designed, interactive book.

FOR ADVANCED READERS (AGES 11+)

Berman, Avis. *James McNeill Whistler.* First Impressions series. New York: Harry N. Abrams, Inc., 1993.
This biography is a thorough introduction to the painter's interesting life and work.

Mühlberger, Richard. *What Makes a Monet a Monet.* New York: The Metropolitan Museum of Art and Viking, 1994.
The life and work of the French painter is explored in an examination that shows children how to recognize the artist's unique style.

Turner, Robyn Montana. *Georgia O'Keeffe.* Portraits of Women Artists for Children series. Boston: Little, Brown and Company, 1991.
The fascinating life of this unique American artist is enriched by many wonderful examples of her paintings. Another title in this series is *Rosa Bonheur,* also by Robyn Montana Turner.

WHERE TO SEE THE ARTISTS' WORK

ROSA BONHEUR

- The Metropolitan Museum of Art, New York
- Musée d'Orsay, Paris
- National Museum of Women in the Arts, Washington, D.C.

CHARLES BURCHFIELD

- Burchfield-Penney Art Center, Buffalo
- Butler Institute of American Art, Youngstown, Ohio
- Charles H. MacNider Museum, Mason City, Iowa
- Miami University Art Museum, Oxford, Florida
- Midwest Museum of American Art, Elkhart, Indiana
- Minnesota Museum of Art, St. Paul
- National Museum of American Art, Smithsonian Institution, Washington, D.C.
- Westmoreland Museum of Art, Greensburg, Pennsylvania

JOHN CONSTABLE

- The Art Institute of Chicago
- The Huntington Library, Art Collection, and Botanical Gardens, San Marino, California
- National Gallery, London
- Philadelphia Museum of Art
- University Center Gallery, Bucknell University, Lewisburg, Pennsylvania
- Victoria and Albert Museum, London

ARTHUR DOVE

- Amon Carter Museum, Fort Worth
- Charles H. MacNider Museum, Mason City, Iowa
- New Jersey Museum, Trenton
- The Phillips Collection, Washington, D.C.
- Carl Van Vechten Gallery of Fine Arts, Fisk University, Nashville
- Wichita Art Museum, Wichita, Kansas

RED GROOMS

- Art Museum of Southeast Texas, Beaumont
- Brooklyn Museum, New York
- Cleveland Center for Contemporary Art
- The Hudson River Museum of Westchester, Yonkers, New York
- Masur Museum of Art, Monroe, Louisiana
- Pennsylvania Academy of the Fine Arts, Philadelphia
- Sawhill Gallery, James Madison University, Harrisonburg, Virginia

MARSDEN HARTLEY

- Addison Gallery of American Art, Phillips Academy, Andover, Massachusetts
- The Art Institute of Chicago
- Florida International University Art Museum, Miami
- Portland Museum of Art, Portland, Maine
- Roswell Museum and Art Center, Roswell, New Mexico
- Terra Museum of American Art, Chicago
- Wichita Art Museum, Wichita, Kansas

DAVID HOCKNEY

- Art Gallery of Ontario, Toronto
- The Art Institute of Chicago
- Los Angeles County Museum of Art
- The Metropolitan Museum of Art, New York
- National Gallery of Art, Washington, D.C.
- Nelson-Atkins Museum of Art, Kansas City
- Philadelphia Museum of Art
- Tate Gallery, London

KATSUSHIKA HOKUSAI

- The Art Institute of Chicago
- Bibliothèque Nationale, Paris
- British Museum, London
- Freer Art Gallery, Smithsonian Institution, Washington, D.C.
- Los Angeles County Museum of Art
- The Metropolitan Museum of Art, New York
- Museum of Fine Arts, Boston
- Tokyo National Museum

CLAUDE MONET

- Birmingham Museum of Art, Birmingham, Alabama
- Dixon Gallery and Gardens, Memphis
- High Museum of Art, Atlanta
- Louvre, Paris
- Mead Art Museum, Amherst College, Amherst, Massachusetts
- The Metropolitan Museum of Art, New York
- Monet House and Museum, Giverny, France
- Musée d'Orsay, Paris
- Musée Marmottan, Paris
- Museum of Fine Arts, Springfield, Massachusetts
- Museum of Modern Art, New York
- North Carolina Museum of Art, Raleigh, North Carolina
- Norton Simon Museum of Art, Pasadena, California
- Philadelphia Museum of Art
- The Saint Louis Art Museum
- Spencer Museum of Art, University of Kansas, Lawrence
- University of Rochester Memorial Art Gallery, Rochester, New York

GEORGIA O'KEEFFE

- Albuquerque Museum of Art, History, and Science, Albuquerque, New Mexico
- Amon Carter Museum, Fort Worth
- The Art Institute of Chicago
- Birmingham Museum of Art, Birmingham, Alabama
- Brooklyn Museum, New York
- Maier Museum of Art, Randolph-Macon Women's College, Lynchburg, Virginia
- Museum of Fine Arts, St. Petersburg, Florida
- National Museum of Women in the Arts, Washington, D.C.
- New Jersey State Museum, Trenton
- The Phillips Collection, Washington, D.C.
- Phoenix Art Museum
- Reynolda House Museum of American Art, Winston-Salem, North Carolina
- The Whitney Museum of American Art, New York

FREDERIC REMINGTON

- Amon Carter Museum, Fort Worth
- Bakersfield Museum of Art, Bakersfield, California
- Buffalo Bill Historical Center, Cody, Wyoming
- Eiteljorg Museum of American Indian and Western Art, Indianapolis
- Gilcrease Museum, Tulsa, Oklahoma
- Palm Springs Desert Museum, Palm Springs, California
- The Rockwell Museum, Corning, New York

THÉO VAN RYSSELBERGHE

- Musée d'Art Moderne, Brussels
- Musée d'Orsay, Paris
- Rijksmuseum Kröller-Müller (Otterlo), the Netherlands

JOSEPH MALLORD WILLIAM TURNER

- Allen Memorial Art Museum, Oberlin College, Oberlin, Ohio
- Cleveland Museum of Art
- Dallas Museum of Art
- The Huntington Library Art Collections and Botanical Gardens, San Marino, California
- Indianapolis Museum of Art
- Museum of Fine Arts, Boston
- National Gallery, London
- Taft Museum, Cincinnati
- Tate Gallery, London
- The Turner Museum, Denver

JAMES ABBOTT McNEILL WHISTLER

- The Art Institute of Chicago
- British Museum, London
- The Detroit Institute of Arts
- Glasgow Art Gallery and Museum
- Solomon R. Guggenheim Museum, New York
- Los Angeles County Museum of Art
- Louvre, Paris
- Museum of Modern Art, New York
- National Gallery of Scotland, Edinburgh
- The Phillips Collection, Washington, D.C.
- Tate Gallery, London

GRANT WOOD

- The Art Institute of Chicago
- Cedar Rapids Museum of Art, Cedar Rapids, Iowa
- Kalamazoo Institute of Arts, Kalamazoo, Michigan
- Lakeview Museum of Arts and Sciences, Peoria, Illinois
- Minnesota Museum of Art, St. Paul
- Reynolda House Museum of American Art, Winston-Salem, North Carolina
- Sheldon Swope Art Museum, Terre Haute, Indiana
- Sioux City Art Center, Sioux City, Iowa
- Spencer Museum of Art, University of Kansas, Lawrence
- Whitney Museum of American Art, New York

N. C. WYETH

- Brandywine River Museum, Chadds Ford, Pennsylvania
- Buffalo Bill Historical Center, Cody, Wyoming
- Eiteljorg Museum of American Indian and Western Art, Indianapolis
- William A. Farnsworth Library and Art Museum, Rockland, Maine
- Charles and Emma Frye Art Museum, Seattle
- Reading Public Museum and Art Gallery, Reading, Pennsylvania

CREDITS *(listed in order of appearance)*

Rosa Bonheur (1822–1899). *Ploughing in the Nivernais Region,* 1849. Oil on canvas, 52¾ × 102⅜ in. (134 × 260 cm), Musée d'Orsay, Paris. Red Grooms (b. 1937). *Ploughed Earth,* 1977. Acrylic on wood, 38¼ × 52 × 3 in. (97.2 × 132.1 × 7.6 cm), Collection of Robert E. Abrams, New York. © 1996 Red Grooms/Artists Rights Society. Grant Wood (1892–1942). *Spring Turning,* 1936. Oil on masonite panel, 18¼ × 40¼ in. (46.4 × 101.6 cm), Reynolda House Museum of American Art, Winston-Salem, North Carolina. © 1996 Estate of Grant Wood/Licensed by VAGA, New York, NY. Marsden Hartley (1877–1943). *Landscape No. 3,* 1920. Oil on canvas, 27¾ × 35¾ in. (70.4 × 90.8 cm), The Art Institute of Chicago. Alfred Stieglitz Collection. Photograph © 1994 The Art Institute of Chicago. All Rights Reserved. N. C. Wyeth (1882–1945). *The Giant,* 1923. Oil on canvas, 72 × 60 in. (182.9 × 15.2 cm), Brandywine River Museum, Chadds Ford, Pa. Collection of Westtown School, Westtown, Pa. Charles E. Burchfield (1893–1967). *Oncoming Spring,* 1954. Watercolor on paper, 30 × 40 in. (76.2 × 101.6 cm), Burchfield-Penney Art Center/The Museum for Western New York Arts, Buffalo. Purchased in part with support from the Western New York Foundation and the Olmsted family in memory of Harold L. Olmsted, 1990:3. John Constable (1776–1837). *Study of Sky and Clouds,* 1821. Oil on paper, 9¾ × 12 in. (24.8 × 30.5 cm), Victoria and Albert Museum, London/Art Resource, New York. Georgia O'Keeffe (1887–1986). *Sky Above Clouds, IV,* 1965. Oil on canvas, 96 × 288 in. (243.8 × 731.5 cm), The Art Institute of Chicago. Restricted gift of the Paul and Gabriella Rosenbaum Foundation, gift of Georgia O'Keeffe. Photograph © 1994 The Art Institute of Chicago. All Rights Reserved. © 1995 The Georgia O'Keeffe Foundation/Artists Rights Society (ARS), New York. Arthur Dove (1880–1946). *Fire in a Sauerkraut Factory,* 1941. Oil on canvas, 10 × 12 in. (25.4 × 30.5 cm). Photograph courtesy of the Terry Dintenfass Gallery, New York. J.M.W. Turner (1775–1851). *The Burning of the Houses of Parliament,* 1834–35. Oil on canvas, 36½ × 48½ in. (92.7 × 123.2 cm), The Cleveland Museum of Art. John L. Severance Collection. Frederic Remington (1861–1909). *Apache Medicine Song,* 1908. Oil on canvas, 27⅛ × 29⅞ in. (68.9 × 75.9 cm), courtesy Sid Richardson Collection of Western Art, Fort Worth, Texas. James Abbott McNeill Whistler (1834–1903). *Nocturne in Black and Gold: Falling Rocket,* c. 1875. Oil on panel, 24¾ × 18¾ in. (62.9 × 47.6 cm), The Detroit Institute of Arts. Katsushika Hokusai (1760–1849). *In the Well of the Great Wave off Kanagawa,* 1823–29. Woodblock print, 10⅛ × 14¹⁵⁄₁₆ in. (26 × 38 cm), The Metropolitan Museum of Art, New York. Théo van Rysselberghe (1862–1926). *The Steersman,* 1892. Oil on canvas, 23⅝ × 31½ in. (60 × 80 cm), Musée d'Orsay, Paris. David Hockney, (b. 1937). *A Bigger Splash,* 1967. Acrylic on canvas, 96 × 96 in. (243.8 × 243.8 cm), © David Hockney. Claude Monet (1840–1926). *Les Nymphéas Blancs (The White Waterlilies),* 1899. Oil on canvas, 35 × 36⅝ in. (89 x 93 cm), Pushkin Museum of Fine Arts, Moscow/Superstock.